PENGUINS in the PEWS:

Climate, Change and Church Growth

J. Russell Crabtree

Penguins in the Pews: *Climate, Change and Church Growth*

Published by MAGI Press.

ISBN 978-0-9977687-3-2

Dedicated to

Dr. Linda Karlovec

Friend and Feather Emeritus

What People Are Saying About Penguins

In Penguins in the Pews: Climate, Change and Church Growth, Russ Crabtree has done it again. Using data collected from over 1300 churches Crabtree convincingly argues that only when congregational leaders address issues of climate and culture will they be able to grow their church. Using a series of charts Crabtree documents what causes a church to decline and what are the must-have characteristics for growth. Discussion helps for church planning teams, middle judicatories and church consultants make this a great tool for any group desiring rebirth in their church. The decades long decline in mainline Christianity is not going to be reversed easily, but in this compact book Russ Crabtree provides a pathway for hope.

Rev. Peter Geisendorfer-Lindgren
Senior Pastor
Lord of Life Lutheran Church

This seminal resource is an extension of Russ Crabtree's life and ministry to revitalize churches. It is a provocative and intelligent wake-up call for clergy and denominational leaders to rethink the nature of church growth. Russ writes with passion and clarity to address key myths, mistaken beliefs, and the social norms that keep churches hard-wired culturally to resist and/or avoid necessary change. His research will take you and your congregation on a journey to reveal the way forward through your unique potential and God-given gifts for growth. His measurable organization intelligence models and process will build consensus and streamline change for leadership teams. With over twenty years of practical research he provides evidence for how clergy and leaders can work to shift church culture climate by using intelligent, systems-thinking data. The outcomes provide leaders with clarity, empowerment, consensus-building, and a focused way to target limited resources for the greatest impact for growing churches that are vital in their communities. I highly recommend this book to bishops, cabinets, judicatory leaders, clergy and anyone else with a passion to implement effective, successful and lasting change.

Rev. Dr. Sharon Barley,
Consultant, Clergy2Lead
Intentional Interim UM Clergy, Eastern Pa Conference

Interest in spirituality and longing for a sense of community has been growing within our culture. And yet, we are not seeing this interest drawing persons for the most part into our churches; in fact we all recognize that, especially for main line churches, regular church attendance is declining. How do we make sense of this? Is it possible that the way we "do" church, the patterns of church life we established and hardly think about, blind us from seeing how elements of our church culture actually prevent persons from finding spiritual healing and spiritual resources within our church communities? Do we often fail to address the issues seekers today face in their lives?

In Penguin in the Pews, Russ Crabtree uses evidenced-based data from over 1300 congregations to reveal why climate and culture shifts are needed in our churches. He points out the alarming statistic that over the past 50 years, membership in most mainline churches has dropped by more than half. Often we are unaware of our own cultural behaviors until a mirror, in the form of data, reveals what is inhibiting our understanding of the shadow sides of our congregational culture. Russ explains that aspects of our church culture that once advanced the church's mission can now lead to the church's demise. Penguin in the Pews will enlighten you on how decreases in both satisfaction and energy have the most detrimental impact on church attendance. If you care about the future of your congregation and transformation of the church, read and use this book and the resources cited in it to become more self-aware. Find out how you can resource your congregation to become energized by the challenges you face in ways that demonstrate creativity, courage, and compassion in the journey toward transformation!

Rev. Sherill Hostetter
Director of Clergy and Congregation Care
Samaritan Center
Lancaster, PA

The insights within these pages make difficult conversations easier and provide clarity in prioritizing resources as middle judicatories engage congregations in renewal, redevelopment, and even closure. Many of our congregations are merely finding ways to survive, and often begin by focusing on membership and finances, a large congregation with an endowment might think they are far from closure and therefore deny decline. They miss incredible opportunities for growth. A small congregation might miss their transforming potential because they focus on numbers. This book gives congregations and middle judicatories insight into where we can best focus our attention so that we can engage in meaningful, powerful ministry based on congregational vitality not numbers. The organization intelligence provides us with an opportunity to engage in creative, innovative, and deeply meaningful faith experiences where congregations thrive rather than merely survive. It is a must read for any congregational leader exploring church growth and decline and will transform your conversations.

The Rev. Sara J. Anderson
Associate to the Bishop
New England Synod, ELCA

Russ Crabtree's book distills his extensive work with congregations and judicatories using organizational Intelligence to discover the factors that can turn decline into new life and growth. With questions for reflection at the end of each chapter for congregational leaders, judicatory leaders and process consultants, it is a rich resource for any church that wants to become more self-aware and intentional in its ministry. It's a small book with profoundly great potential for congregations and all the people who care about them. I would have liked to have it to share with the congregations in my presbyteries.

Paige M. McRight
Retired Executive Presbyter for Central Florida and North Alabama Presbyteries in the Presbyterian Church USA

Russ Crabtree's work in applying organizational intelligence toward the cultural architecture of the church is nothing short of manna. While many of us pastors are engaged in the very hard work of transforming congregational culture, we often lack the organizational awareness, experience and skill sets to gather, interpret, and apply relevant data. Penguins in the Pews provides hands on tools for asking the right questions and pointing leaders toward a healthy pathway that can bear fruit for congregational development. This book should be required reading for everyone engaged in congregational leadership.

Rev. Dr. Douglas A. Hill
Lead Pastor
Abiding Hope Church

Acknowledgements

In the acknowledgements for Owl Sight, I indicated that the book had roughly 50,000 contributors. For this book, that number has grown to nearly 200,000 persons from more than 1,300 churches. As was the case then, the vast majority must remain unnamed because the contribution was an anonymous, though very personal, sharing of their thoughts through a series of questions they chose to answer. This makes it difficult to speak in any possessive way about the discoveries in this book. As I keep saying, it is not so much what I have discovered, but what we have discovered together.

However, a few names are important to mention. I want to thank Susan Niemi of Huff Publishing Associates for ably editing this book. She makes me a better author and offers the reader a clearer message. I also want to thank Heather Clark for the terrific cover and book design.

It is always important to have the support of critical thinkers who will read early versions of a manuscript, make valuable suggestions, and then take their place squarely in your corner. These precious folks include Michelle Snyder and Robyn Strain. I am strengthened as I bring them to mind.

A special thanks goes to Emily Swanson who continues to make the Holy Cow! Consulting database available for this research.

Thanks also to my wife, Shawn, for her emotional support combined with the very practical gift of proofreading the manuscript.

When I think that all these gifts are expressions of the pure grace of God, I run out of words.

PENGUINS in the PEWS:

Climate, Change and Church Growth

Contents

Preface

The genesis of this book can be traced to an article I read on the fifty-year decline in populations of emperor penguins attributed to the disappearance of sea ice in Antarctica. This led to a reflection on the similarities between the way the United States is dealing with climate change and the way the mainline church is dealing with its own decline. **It is a good example of how denial spans the political and social spectrum.**

We are living in a society that is significantly counterfactual in its thinking.

At both the policy and popular level, there is often a wide gap between what is known with virtual certainty as fact among scientists and what is acknowledged to be true in the rest of society. In 2016 more than 2,300 American scientists, including 22 Nobel Prize winners, issued an open letter to President-elect Donald Trump and Congress, urging them to respect science. They are especially worried about government interference in their work and about policies that could reject scientific fact.[1]

While the public is largely positive about the value of science to make life better[2], there is a wide gap between what people believe on specific issues and what has been established as scientific fact. This gap leads to some interesting contradictions. People who rely every day on extremely sophisticated scientific technologies like computers and GPS often reject the findings of that same scientific approach regarding issues like climate change and vaccinations. As a society we are a bit like folks who drive horse and buggy, but nonetheless use cell phones.

I would put these particular forms of denial in the more

conservative column. However, progressives have their own stubborn resistance to facts, not necessarily to data from the physical sciences, but to data about the effectiveness of the systems they maintain, often with ferocity. We see this in education. The United States spends more per student than any other country in the world. Despite this, US students still trail their rivals on international tests.[3]

Yet progressives will often align themselves with a position that schools simply need more tax dollars. This, too, is a form of denial.

It is no secret that the mainline church in the United States has been declining in membership and influence for more than fifty years. While this decline can be easily established by simple count data such as membership and worship attendance, the history of responses to that data is replete with diversions and rationalizations of various kinds. One of the most common is the assertion that while the quantity of members in mainline churches has declined, the quality of church life has remained high.

With the advent of organizational intelligence, we know that is simply not true. Most mainline churches are losing members, and the churches losing the most are those where members indicate significant problems with their experiences in those congregations. As a group, the only churches that are growing are those where people indicate very positive experiences, perhaps the abundant life that Jesus promised.[4]

What is notable is the silence of denominational leaders regarding the organizational intelligence emerging out of their own churches. One might think the realization that only 50 percent of the members of a typical congregation are clearly satisfied with their church and 37 percent generally agree that their church is "going through the motions" would generate a significant conversation. It is a fact that the longer members stay in a typical mainline church, the more disillusioned they become. This is a terrible indictment of the status quo. Yet denominational leaders are largely silent. Whether penguins or Protestants, the way that we are dealing with their disappearance is not all that different. **Conservatives and progressives alike are simply avoiding change and piping to complacency.**

I hold the church to a higher standard than the other institutions of our society. The unwillingness of the church to deal with the facts of its own existence sets a poor example for the rest of us.

Invariably, leaders will say that they are trying to maintain morale by highlighting the positive. "What is to be gained by focusing on deficits?" they ask me.

Here is my response: What we gain by facing the truth are the same things we gain by focusing on any hard problem—the generation of creativity, innovation, and motivation for change. John Kennedy elicited these qualities from the nation when he said in his speech at Rice University:

> **We choose to go to the moon in this decade and do the other things, not because they are easy, but because they are hard, because that goal will serve to organize and measure the best of our energies and skills, because that challenge is one that we are wiling to accept, one we are unwilling to postpone, and one which we intend to win.**[5]

That was not a new thought. Jesus said the path to an abundant life was one that led down a difficult road. People lie down before illusions. They rise up before worthy challenges.

The good news is there are churches that are offering their members transformative experiences within the Body of

Christ. The good news is that these same churches are likely to be growing. The additional good news is that these same churches are being energized by the challenges they face in ways that demonstrate creativity, courage, and compassion.

Perhaps there is no more difficult, more important, or more inspiring challenge than this for the church of Jesus Christ in the twenty-first century.

---

1 http://www.nbcnews.com/health/health-news/worried-scientists-urge-trump-respect-their-work-n690426

2 https://www.theatlantic.com/health/archive/2015/01/americans-believe-in-science-just-not-its-findings/384937/

3 http://www.cbsnews.com/news/us-education-spending-tops-global-list-study-shows/

4 John 10:10

5 https://er.jsc.nasa.gov/seh/ricetalk.htm

Introduction

In a study published in *Nature,* scientists showed that over the past fifty years the numbers of emperor penguins in Antarctica have dropped by more than 50 percent.[6]

The problem: The current climate cannot support penguin populations, and emperor penguins in particular are having trouble adapting to the change.

Eight thousand miles to the north, a similar problem is devastating populations of Protestants where, over the past fifty years, membership in most mainline churches has dropped by more than half. The problem: Like their penguin cousins, the current climate in most churches does not offer a compelling reason to belong, and members are having trouble adapting to the change.

Members realize that something must be done. When nearly 200,000 members from more than 1,300 churches were asked where they would like the church to invest additional energy, they prioritized "develop a comprehensive plan to reach new members" as the first or second priority 92 percent of the time. With the median age more than fifty-three years, the members of the typical mainline church are significantly older than the general population. Conscious of the demographic hole for younger cohorts in their congregations, 72 percent of churches ranked "make necessary changes to reach families with children and youth" as first or second as well.

The concern for numeric growth is undoubtedly a response to nearly fifty years of membership decline in mainline denominational churches. A review of the last ten years of data from the churches in the Holy Cow! Consulting database reveals that this decline continues, and it is universal across all denominations (figure 1).

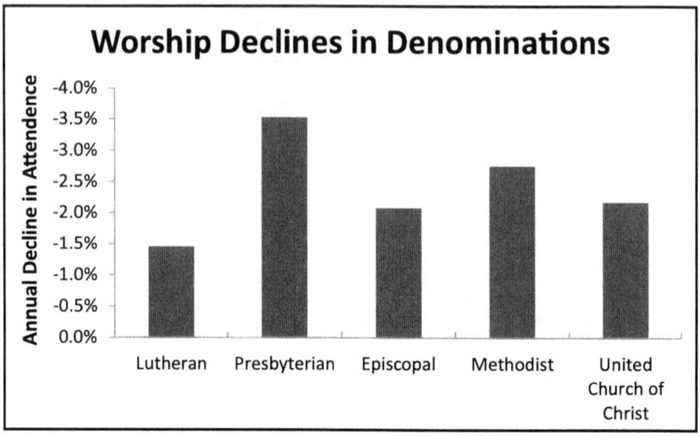

Figure 1: Decline in Attendance Universal for Mainline Churches

Congregational leaders are looking for resources that can help them address these priorities. When 20,000 leaders were asked where they wanted their middle judicatory to invest additional energy, "equipping leaders to reach new members" was the first or second priority 100 percent of the time. Given the opportunity, it is reasonable to assume that leaders would prioritize services from church consultants in a similar order.

Over the years, leaders have adopted a number of different perspectives on this decline as they guide churches.

In some quarters, it has been treated as a nonissue. From this perspective, churches are called to be faithful. Numeric growth or decline is in God's hands. The advantage of this approach is that it frees leaders from the complexities involved in making new disciples and allows them to focus solely on issues bubbling up in the corporate consciousness.

A related approach has been to treat numeric decline as beneficial. The thought is that many persons who joined the church in the fifties and sixties were members in name only. Their departure from the church has left a core of more committed members who can now be about a ministry unhampered by the inertia of halfheartedness.

A third approach has been to treat numeric growth as a by-product of church vitality. If a church is healthy, it will automatically grow. If a church is not growing, it is a sign that something is internally amiss. This approach allows members to simply focus on the health of the church with the assumption that numeric growth will follow.

A fourth approach has been to engage the issue of church growth directly through programs that have a proven track record in other faith communities. What one church can do, another can do. The advantage of this approach is that it offers clarity through a set of programmatic blueprints.

An alternative approach is what I call an *intelligent system growth strategy.* In contrast to the perspectives above, this strategy is built on four core affirmations.

- Church growth is the result of a core commitment to making disciples, whether understood as individual salvation or incorporation into a soul-saving community.
- Church growth is ecological in nature. An unhealthy church environment tends to foster a decline in numbers rather than growth. The churches that are losing members at the fastest rates are those that are the least healthy.
- Church growth occurs when strategies are employed that are tailored to a particular context. Programs adopted from other churches without consideration of climate and culture will generally fail.
- Church growth strategies benefit from organizational intelligence, made possible by information technology, which provides valuable insights that can clarify factors that impede or enhance church growth.

An intelligent system growth strategy is an intentional, evidence-based effort to create and optimize these environments for growth. More about what I mean by an intelligent system is in the next chapter.

This book is written for leaders at every level.

This book is for church leaders serving on planning teams of various kinds, most of whom serve churches with members who indicate that reaching new people is their highest priority. This includes teams involved in planning for a pastoral transition. The best time for developing a church growth strategy is when that strategy can shape the transition plan of the church and the desired profile for the next pastor.

This book is for the regional association leaders, conferences, dioceses, synods, presbyteries, and districts who are being asked by local leaders to make "equipping leaders to reach new members" their highest priority.

This book is for professional church consultants who shoulder the responsibility of guiding churches in directions that are both faithful and fruitful.

Much of this book is built on the approach detailed in the book *Owl Sight: Evidence-Based Discernment and the Promise of Organizational Intelligence.*[7] Readers will find Owl Sight to be a helpful preface to this one.

Discussion Questions for Planning Teams

1. Think of a time when you had an experience that affected how often you attended worship. Describe that experience.
2. In what way is your church like the emperor penguins described at the beginning of this introduction?
3. Review the four approaches to church growth found in this introduction. Which perspective

is most common among your members?

4. Do you believe the climate of a church (how people experience it) is more important to folks who are visiting a church today than it was in the past? Why do you think that is?
5. What steps has your church taken to date to reach new people? How are those consistent or inconsistent with an intelligent growth strategy described in this introduction?

Discussion Questions for Middle Judicatory Leaders

1. What is your middle judicatory's perspective on church growth? If you do not have a clear perspective, why or why not?
2. Equipping congregations to reach new members is the highest priority for middle judicatories expressed by local church leaders. What are the obstacles to adopting this as a priority for your middle judicatory?
3. How is your middle judicatory currently responding to that need?
4. What is your middle judicatory currently focused on that is hampering its efforts/desire to help develop vital, viable congregations?

Reflection for Consultants

1. What approach to church growth do you use in your work with congregations?

2. How do you customize your approach to church growth for churches in a variety of contexts?
3. What is the most difficult part of designing a customized approach?
4. How do you currently assess the climate and culture of a church you are working with?

---

6 *http://abcnews.go.com/Technology/story?id=98565&page=1*

7 *Crabtree, J. Russell, Owl Sight, Evidence-Based Discernment and the Promise of Organizational Intelligence for Ministry (Magi Press, 2012)*

Chapter 1

Intelligent Systems

What is an intelligent system?

It has nothing to do with the level of education or aptitude of individual members. Churches with highly educated members can fail to respond as intelligent systems. So what is it?

An intelligent system is one where members are aware of their own patterned, group behavior. The opposite of an intelligent church is not a stupid church—it is an unaware church.

Jesus identified a lack of self-awareness as a major issue. The famous dictum "Do not judge, so that you may not be judged"[8] is not really a prohibition against judging. It is a call to address a deficient level of self-awareness that is blind to the log in one's own eye and obstructs the ability to remove the splinter in the eye of another. Jesus was not diminishing the value of feedback to another, which can be extremely helpful. He was pointing out that a lack of self-awareness compromises the ability to do meaningful ministry.

Jesus also addressed a lack of self-awareness through the metaphor of blindness. In John 9, the Pharisees asked Jesus, "Surely, we are not blind, are we?"[9]

Jesus replied, "If you were blind you would not have sin. But now that you say, 'We see,' your sin remains."[10] Jesus used the plural of the pronoun you that means he was addressing "group blindness." Entire groups can lack self-awareness of their own patterned behaviors. The apostle Paul addressed this problem in the early church (1 Corinthians 4:8), as did John the revelator (Revelation 3:17).

Members of a faith community engage in patterned behavior all the time. Bob, Mary, and George will (predictably) be upset if the service runs late. Boyd will (predictably) complain about children making noise in the service. Mike and Susan will (predictably) love the music when all the stops are pulled out on the Casavant organ.

When aggregated over all the members, this patterned behavior creates a *climate* within the church that folks experience as positive or negative. Church climate is much like the meteorological climate we experience where we live. It can be cold, stormy, balmy, or changeable. In some climates neither penguins nor church members can easily survive.

When I worked at the Eastman Kodak Company, I was asked to help recruit other professionals to the company. In that process, I discovered that the number one reason people declined to accept a job offer to Kodak was the climate in Rochester, New York. In the same way that people consider climate in making a decision about where to live, people consider church climate in choosing a faith community. Think of a church struggling with conflict as one with a climate of constant rain and emotional lightning strikes.

Patterned behavior also creates an *organizational culture* in churches. Organizational culture is best described as a set of reflexes that are neither positive nor negative in themselves. This is observed at the most practical level as folks enter a worship space and decide where to sit, usually near a spot where they have sat for weeks or months previously. This patterned behavior is also observed in how members respond to change and how they react to theological questions.

The way a member of an Episcopal church responds to a theological discussion about baptism will be predictably different from how a Baptist will respond.

Organizational culture creates a kind of operating system. Just like a particular app may not be compatible with the operating system of your phone, church growth programs that work in one church may not work in another.

An intelligent church is one where members are aware of the climate and culture within their congregation. It is impossible to develop a meaningful growth strategy without this level of awareness.

Getting Smart about Climate and Culture

Most leaders do not have a way to identify the climate and culture within their churches. The information they have is what I call count data.

Count data is information that can be obtained by simply counting people or things. Financial revenue, average worship attendance, and membership rolls are all count data.

Count data has two shortcomings. First, count data is a downstream metric. Changes in count data (like worship attendance) are generally downstream from changes in the experiences of members. A church can be growing numerically while accumulating a backlog of discontent that will eventually poison the spirit of the church and arrest further growth. The negative aspects of the system get baked in. By the time count data reflects this, the damage has been done, sometimes without remedy.

The second and more significant shortcoming of count data is that it can't be used to discover the climate or culture of a congregation. This requires *witness data*. Witness data is information that can only be gathered when a person speaks, either in a narrative or a symbolic form using numbers to represent the intensity of thoughts and feelings.

Intelligent Systems and Climate MAPs

As discussed earlier, the members of faith communities engage in patterned behaviors. These behaviors are rooted in their attitudes. A shorthand way of referring to a particular pattern is through the acronym MAP, **M**ember **A**ttitudinal **P**attern. Whereas count data is best represented by numbers, climate and culture are best represented by images.

A climate MAP is one that uses an image to represent the patterned attitudes of members toward one or more aspects of their experience in the church. One example of a climate MAP is the Energy-Satisfaction MAP (figure 2).

The Energy-Satisfaction MAP locates the climate of a church in one of four states.

(1) CHAOS: low satisfaction and high energy

(2) RECOVERY: low satisfaction and low energy

(3) STATIC: high satisfaction and low energy

(4) TRANSFORMATIONAL: high satisfaction and high energy

Whereas count data aims to deliver information in the form of numbers, the goal of a MAP is to provide a kind of Cliff Notes narrative describing some aspect of the climate of a church.

For example, members of a church in the CHAOS quadrant are experiencing a church with substantial energy and purpose, but one that may be struggling to know how to align the various aspects of its ministries to a common purpose. Confusion about ways to achieve goals or the vying of various groups for resources or power can generate a climate of uncertainty or even power struggles.

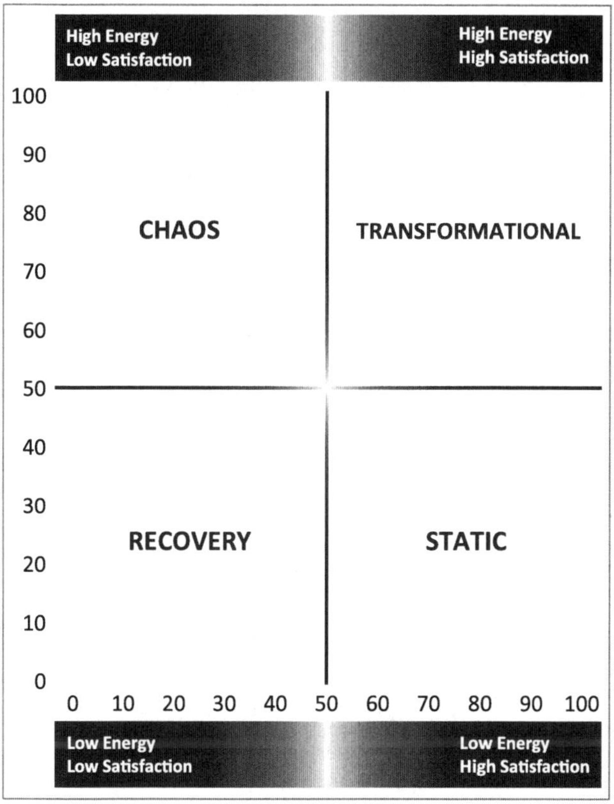

Figure 2 Climate MAP: Energy-Satisfaction

Members of a church in the TRANSFORMATIONAL quadrant are experiencing a relatively high level of vitality in their congregation. This level of vitality offers the church a number of strategic options including growth, expansion of ministry or facilities, replication, or increased external impact. These outcomes are not guaranteed, but are real possibilities if the church continues to take risks and adopts the appropriate strategies.

Members of a church in the RECOVERY quadrant can imagine a church more vital than they are currently experiencing. Somewhat lower levels of satisfaction can be motivating for change as long as members have a clear sense of direction and some concrete, first steps to take, and they are willing to contribute to the change instead of simply waiting for others to change.

Finally, members of a church in the STATIC quadrant have a deep appreciation for the life they share as a congregation. However, they may find it difficult to muster the energy required to make changes that are critical to their future. If reigniting a sense of purpose is not a realistic option, it may be necessary to add ministries without putting additional demands on current members.

As will be discussed in the next chapter, each of these regions of the MAP offers different propensities for growth or decline. Before a growth strategy can be developed, leaders must know where their church is located on this MAP.

Intelligent Systems and Culture MAPs

A culture MAP is one that uses an image to represent the organizational reflexes of members. One example is the Descriptive MAP (figure 3).

The Descriptive MAP locates the culture of a church in one of four different operating systems.

(1) MAGI: theologically progressive and adaptable

(2) PARACLETE: theologically progressive and settled

(3) HEARTH AND HOME: theologically conservative and settled

(4) PERFORMANCE: theologically conservative and adaptable

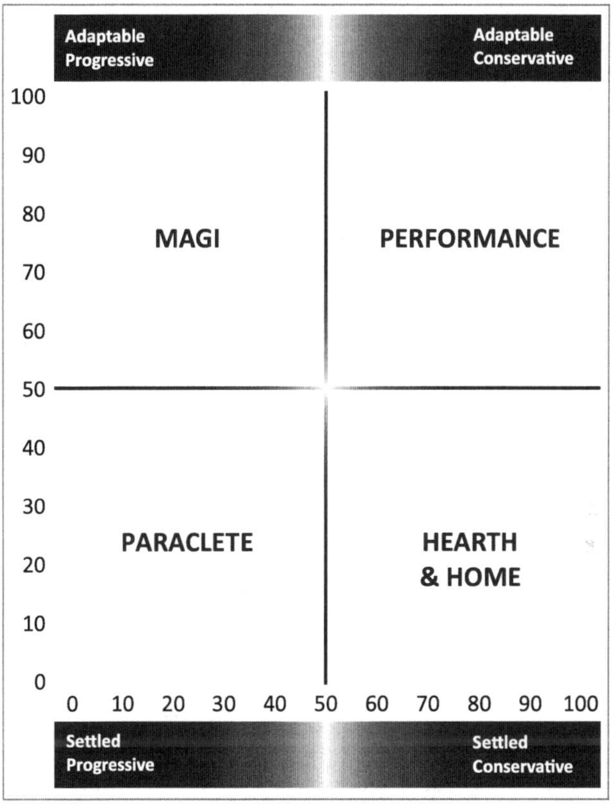

Figure 3 Descriptive MAP: Flexibility-Theological Perspective

Again, locating a congregation on this MAP provides a snippet of the church's story.

Members of a MAGI culture church are likely to embrace changes from time to time, either because they enjoy variety or they know that change is necessary to reach a changing society. On average, the church is theologically more progressive. The combination of an adaptable approach to change and a more progressive theological perspective gives the church potential strengths that include curiosity, advocacy, and inclusiveness. On the other hand, the church may find it difficult to develop a clear and compelling vision for its future and may rely too heavily upon reason to generate enthusiasm.

Members of a PERFORMANCE culture church are likely to embrace changes from time to time, either because they enjoy variety or believe that change is necessary to reach a changing society. On average, the church is theologically more conservative. The combination of an adaptable approach to change and a more conservative theological perspective gives the church potential strengths in the areas of relevance, religious experience, and spiritual/moral clarity. On the other hand, the church may find it difficult to engage the difficult issues that do not go away upon conversion and sometimes erupt without warning. They may also find themselves experiencing a religious high but without roots that lead to sustainable change.

Members of a PARACLETE culture church like to find familiar ways of doing things and stick with them. On average, the church is theologically more progressive. The combination of a settled approach to change and a more progressive theological perspective gives the church potential strengths that can include compassion, healing, and service to others. On the other hand, the church may find itself overly suspicious of religious experience. Without a commitment to transformation, members may also overcommit to meeting the needs of others to the extent that it suffers burnout and a loss of conviction about the difference it is making.

Members of a HEARTH AND HOME culture church like to find familiar ways of doing things and stick with them. On average, the church is theologically more conservative. The combination of a settled approach to change and a more conservative theological perspective gives the church potential strengths in the areas of moral and spiritual clarity; stability in the face of chaotic, societal change; and maintenance of important traditions. On the other hand, the church may find it difficult to make the changes required to achieve its goals without triggering debilitating conflicts.

The next chapter will focus on the tendencies of churches in different regions of this MAP to grow or decline.

Discussion Questions for Planning Teams

1. What makes it difficult for a church or individual to admit that they might not be self-aware?
2. How self-aware do you believe your congregation is of its climate and culture?
3. What count data does your church regularly collect? What data on climate and culture does your church regularly collect?
4. As individuals in the group, place a mark on the area of the Energy-Satisfaction MAP that best describes your church climate. Discuss areas of agreement and difference.
5. As individuals in the group, place a mark on the area of the Descriptive MAP that best describes your church culture. Discuss areas of agreement and difference.

Discussion Questions for Middle Judicatory Leaders

1. How self-aware do you believe the churches are in your middle judicatory?
2. If you were to place the churches of your middle judicatory on the grids in this chapter, how confident would you feel in their accuracy?
3. How big a gap is there between your perception of churches and their own self-awareness?

4. Reflect on the churches that you have interacted with in the last month. Where do you think they are on these MAPS? How would you advise them regarding their desire to grow? What criteria would you use to advise them?
5. Would it be helpful to know where the most concentrated needs are in your middle judicatory?

Reflection for Consultants

1. How self-aware do you believe the churches are that you work with?
2. If you were to place the churches you are now working with on the grids in this chapter, how confident would you feel in their accuracy?
3. How big a gap is there between your perception of the churches you are working with and their own self-awareness?
4. Reflect on the churches that you have interacted with in the last month. Where do you think they are on these MAPS? How would you advise them regarding their desire to grow? What criteria would you use to advise them?

---

8 Matthew 7:1

9 John 9:40

10 John 9:41

Chapter 2

Climate and Growth

We know how a climate that is too warm impacts emperor penguins: They begin to disappear. What happens to Protestant Christians when the climate changes? The impact is dramatic.

Here is a story of two churches, St. Luke Episcopal and Morningside Lutheran. Both have good, but typical pastors, both have similar facilities. Both are in the same community. Even though both have made reaching new people a priority, the community is declining in population. As a result, both are seeing a decline in worship attendance. However, Morningside Lutheran is losing attendees at a rate that is *nine times* that of St. Luke Episcopal. As a result, Morningside is going to lose nearly half of its membership in about twelve years and will no longer be able to afford a full-time pastor. During that same period of time, St. Luke will hardly be affected.

Why is one congregation being pushed toward extinction and the other isn't? Climate.

Morningside is in the RECOVERY quadrant of the Climate MAP (figure 2). Members have a low level of satisfaction as well as a lack of enthusiasm for their life together. St. Luke is in the TRANSFORMATIONAL quadrant of the Climate MAP. While members have average levels of satisfaction with the church, they have a high level of energy and enthusiasm for their mission.

Members at Morningside Lutheran look at St. Luke Episcopal and wonder how they do it. "Why are they doing so well and we aren't?" They do not realize that the climate in their church is having such a negative impact because they don't have the information they need to be an intelligent system. Again, the opposite of an intelligent system is not stupidity; it is a lack of self-awareness.

The MAP that follows shows the average four-year worship attendance change for different climates (figure 4).

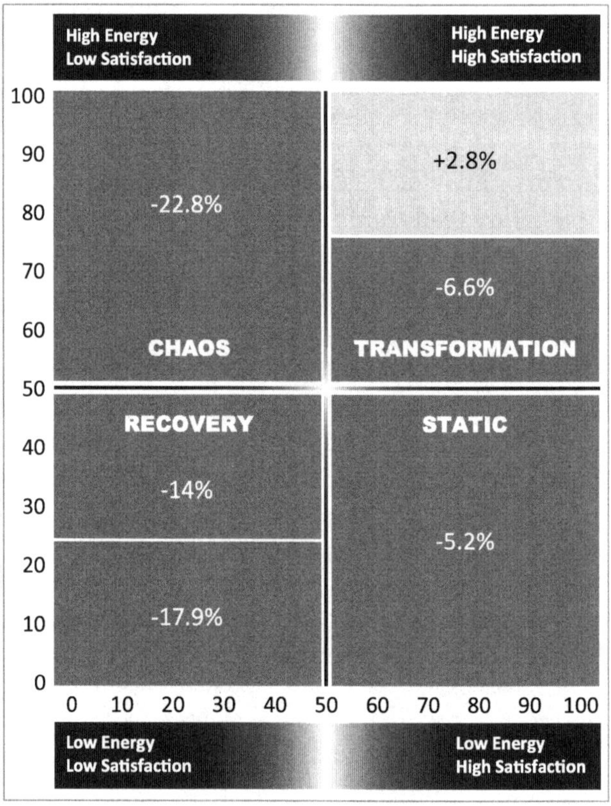

Figure 4 Rates of Growth and Decline for Different Climates

There are a number of observations to be made from this MAP.

First, there is a clear relationship between church climate and changes in worship attendance. Specifically, there is significant downward pressure on worship attendance as levels of either satisfaction or energy decrease. Decreases in satisfaction while maintaining high energy have the most detrimental effect on worship attendance. The distinction between quantity and quality is not valid. Churches with a low-quality climate are likely to end up with low quantities of members.

Second, only churches experiencing higher levels of energy and satisfaction exhibit growth as a group. Even here, the annual rate of growth in worship attendance is small, under 1 percent per year. Chaos, recovery, and static quadrants all exhibit declines in worship attendance as a group.

Third, it is not enough for members to feel generally positive about their churches. They must be raving fans. This means that 70 percent of the members must *clearly* agree that they feel positive about the church. Leaders fall into a trap when they adopt a political perspective in reading climate data. While an approval rating of 51 percent might get a president reelected, it is not enough to generate the level of energy in a church required for growth.

Fourth, while a positive climate doesn't guarantee that a church will grow, a negative climate almost guarantees that it won't. Roughly 55 percent of churches with energy and satisfaction at these high levels are growing. This suggests that a positive climate provides options for growth given the right strategies. It is not the case that a healthy church automatically grows.

On the other hand, 85 percent of churches with low satisfaction and energy are experiencing declines in worship attendance. It is very difficult to develop effective growth strategies in a church with a mediocre climate.

Finally, churches in CHAOS are the most vulnerable to

attendance losses. Groups vying for power or resources are a bigger threat than the low morale experienced by churches in the RECOVERY quadrant.

One question this raises is whether a positive climate contributes to growth or whether growth makes people feel more positive about the climate. To resolve this, I am introducing a second climate MAP, the Hospitality-Focus MAP (figure 5).

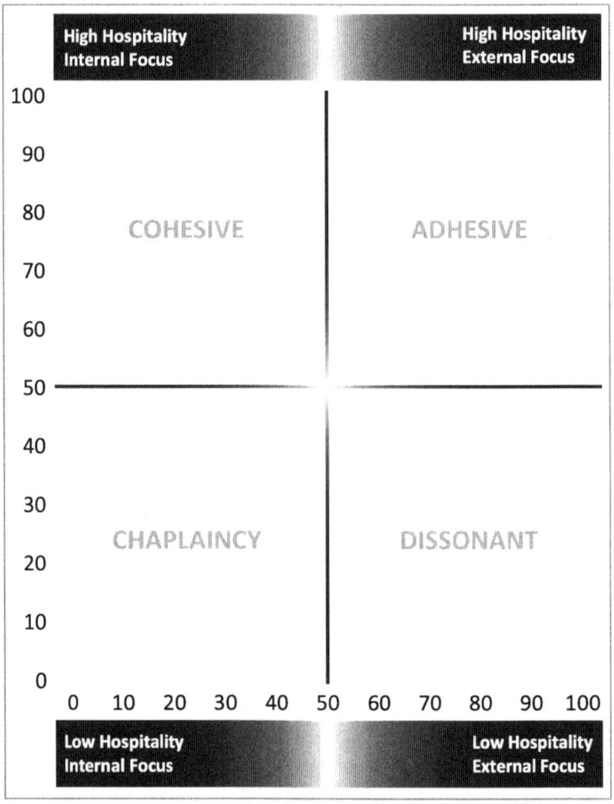

Figure 5 Climate MAP: Hospitality-Focus

The Hospitality-Focus MAP locates the climate of a church in one of four additional states.

(1) COHESIVE: high hospitality with an internal focus

(2) ADHESIVE: high hospitality with an external focus

(3) DISSONANT: low hospitality with an external focus

(4) CHAPLAINCY: low hospitality with an internal focus

In a COHESIVE climate, the internal relationships within the church are relatively strong. However, it may be that the church is more prepared to invest in sustaining those relationships than in risking the conflict that might accompany the changes required to reach persons in the community.

In an ADHESIVE climate, the internal relationships within the church are relatively strong. The church also has a healthy external focus with a willingness to make changes to meet the needs of persons they want to reach in their community.

In a CHAPLAINCY climate, the internal relationships within the church are comparatively weak. In addition, the church does not appear to be making changes designed to meet the needs of people they want to reach in their community. Since members do not take care of one another, the entire burden for care generally falls on an individual, often the pastor.

In a DISSONANT climate, the church has experience in making changes to meet the needs of persons they want to reach in the community. However, the internal relationships within the church are comparatively weak. As a result it may be difficult to retain those the church is able to reach.

Now see how each of these climates exhibits tendencies to grow or decline (figure 6).

Again, there is a clear relationship between church climate and changes in worship attendance. Specifically, there is significant downward pressure on worship attendance as levels of either hospitality or external focus decrease. Decreases in *both* hospitality and external focus (to an internal focus) have the most detrimental impact on worship attendance with declines exceeding 4 percent per year.

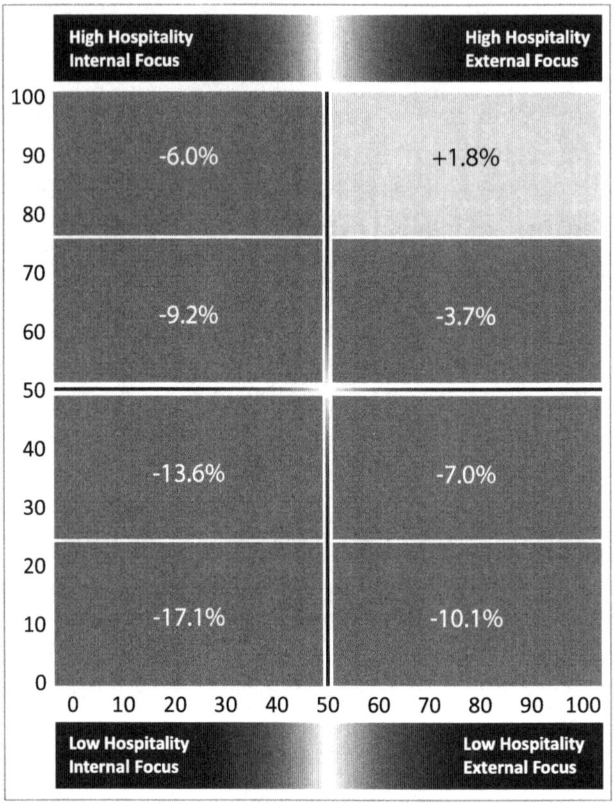

Figure 6 Growth and Decline for Different Climates

Second, only churches experiencing higher levels of hospitality and an external focus exhibit growth as a group. When it comes to growth, it is not enough for a church to be caring. It must be externally focused. And, again, members must be raving fans of the hospitality experienced in the church, rating it higher than 75 percent of the churches in a typical community.

Third, churches that are both internally focused *and* experiencing low hospitality are seeing the largest declines in worship attendance. About 87 percent of churches with this climate are indicating declines in average attendance. Over a ten-year period of time, these churches can expect to lose about a third of their active members. For many congregations, that will drop them below the threshold of viability.

Finally, having an externally focused, hospitable church does not guarantee that a church will grow, but having an internally focused, inhospitable church almost guarantees that it won't. About half of the most hospitable, externally focused churches are growing. Again, this suggests that positive hospitality provides a foundation for growth strategies that must be customized to a particular situation.

An externally focused church is one that is willing to make adjustments to its worship service in order to meet the needs of the persons in the community it wants to reach. It requires a significant, intentional effort on the part of the leadership to shape a congregation that is willing to embrace these changes. It is less reasonable to assume that a growing worship service will automatically become more open to change. In other words, externally focused, hospitable congregations tend to generate growth. Growth doesn't make a church friendlier or more focused on their community.

The next chapter will address what it takes to shift climate.

Discussion Questions for Planning Teams

1. Make a list of five or six organizations (other than the church) where your members voluntarily choose to spend some of their free time. How would they describe the climate in those organizations? How do people tend to respond when organizations have a negative climate?
2. Working as individuals, place a mark on the two MAPS in this chapter that describe the climate of your church. Share those with one another. Where are they the same? Where are they different? Why do you think there might be differences?
3. What does your location on these two MAPS suggest about the likely success or disappointment in efforts to grow the church?
4. When you think about creating a congregation of "raving fans" which of the words below best describe how it makes you feel?
    - Excited
    - Overwhelmed
    - Focused
    - Discouraged

Discussion Questions for Middle Judicatory Leaders

1. Think of three churches that you have interacted with in the last several weeks. If you knew where they were on these two climate MAPS, what would be the impact on:
2. How you interacted with them.
3. How much time you spent with them.
4. What kinds of resources you made available to them.
5. Think of the climate of your middle judicatory. Where would you locate your middle judicatory on these two MAPS? Why might it be important to know that?

Reflection for Consultants

1. Think of three churches that you have interacted with in the last several weeks. If you knew where they were on these two climate MAPS, what would be the impact on:
2. How you interacted with them.
3. How much time you spent with them.
4. What kinds of resources you made available to them.
5. What do you think are the four or five critical factors for a church to create raving fan members?

Chapter 3

Improving Climate

When people hear that the penguins are disappearing because the climate is changing, they often react with denial. In my experience with mainline churches, the response over the first thirty years of decline had a similar ring to it.

"We are only losing dead wood."

"Financial giving is going up, so commitment is strong."

"We're baptizing a lot of children, which is good news for the future."

"We're into quality, not quantity."

As we have seen, the quality versus quantity argument is not valid. As a rule, a decline in the quality of the life of a congregation leads to a decline in the quantity of those involved, plain and simple.

When folks are confronted with this information, they suddenly flip from denial . . . it's not really happening . . . to helplessness . . . there's nothing we can do about it! The good news is that there is something that can be done about it.

Church climate can be changed.

The Story of Three Churches

The churches in figure 7 represent real congregations that have been assigned generic names. Climate has been tracked in each one over a period of three to five years. Worship attendance has been tracked as well.

From 2007 to 2011, First Church's climate changed from deep in the RECOVERY quadrant to near the top of the TRANSFORMATIONAL quadrant. During that period of time, the four-year worship attendance trend changed from -28 percent to +13 percent. I have conducted a study of this church and now know the factors that contributed to these changes.

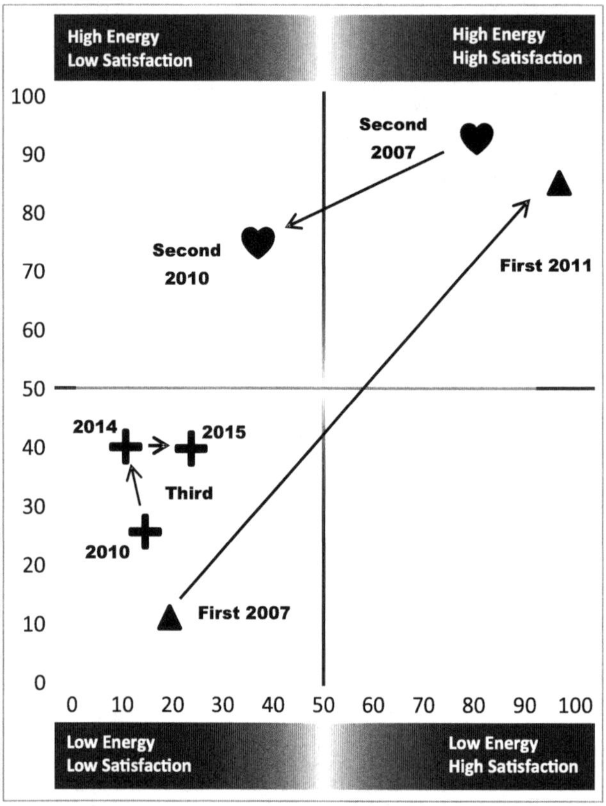

Figure 7 The Effect of Climate Change in Three Congregations

Church climate can also erode. From 2007 to 2010, Second Church's climate changed from TRANSFORMATIONAL to CHAOS. The four-year worship trend dropped from +27 percent to +8 percent. Again, the factors that led to this decline are apparent in the organizational intelligence.

Finally, churches can "wander in the desert." Third Church has remained in the RECOVERY quadrant for more than five years. In the three climate assessments, its four-year worship attendance trend has been -18 percent, -11 percent, and -12 percent.

What makes the difference between a church with positive or improving climate and those with a depressed or eroding climate? The only way to find out is to ask them! However, we don't know whom to talk to if we don't create intelligent systems through the collection of organizational intelligence.

Shifting Climate: Thermometers and Thermostats

When the climate in our homes becomes uncomfortable, we have ways of changing that using a combination of thermometers and thermostats. Both have an important role to play.

Thermometers measure the current state of an environment. When we are feeling too hot or too cold in our home, the first thing we do is check the thermometer to see what the actual temperature is. We may discover that it is not as hot or cold as we think it is and do nothing.

Organizational intelligence is the thermometer of a church's climate. Various individuals may have differing opinions about whether it is warm or chilly. In an intelligent system, that question is settled by looking at the information generated through an assessment.

In many cases, simply having a thermometer is not enough. A change is needed. Now a different mechanism is required: a thermostat. A thermostat has the capacity to change the climate to a desired level. In a church, a thermostat is created through the collective efforts of leaders to improve the experience that members are having in the church.

How does that happen?

Critical Success Factors

One of the most important decisions for leaders who want to improve the climate within their congregations is where to focus their attention. There is a human tendency to define a problem by the least energy solution. At the social level, this tendency is seen in the oppression of minorities. If minorities are defined as the problem, the majority doesn't have to do anything to change. At the church level, it is seen in the avoidance of difficult issues.

Jesus addressed this tendency in the Sermon on the Mount when he insisted that righteousness before God was not simply a matter of avoiding certain behaviors, but of cultivating an inner disposition. For Jesus, it was not enough to simply obey the commandment "do not kill." The disciple must go further and deal with the inner rage from which violent behavior springs.

Church climates are generally not improved by programs that are relatively easy to administer but may not get to the heart of the issue. Getting members to wear name tags is not the ultimate goal of hospitality. The goal of hospitality is to nurture a corporate disposition in members that tunes into the needs of those outside the circle of the congregation and responds with creative compassion.

A critical success factor is an element in the life of a congregation that is important to members and is in need of improvement. There are a number of ways to discover those factors, ranging from focus groups to assessment tools.

Critical success factors vary greatly from one church to another, and to some extent, from one denomination to another. For example, the critical success factors for a typical Episcopal church, framed as goals are:

Success Factor #1	We will create a church where worship experiences are exceptional in their ability to inspire, engage, and enrich our spiritual lives.
Success Factor #2	We will create a church experience where involvement is good for the soul instead of leading to disillusionment or disappointment.
Success Factor #3	We will create a church experience where every person understands the significance of his or her life in the universe and is supported in fulfilling the purpose for which they were born.
Success Factor #4	We will create a church experience where people live in peace with one another by resolving conflict in ways that are respectful and restorative.
Success Factor #5	We will create a church where persons experience leaders who listen deeply with open hearts and make courageous decisions with good intentions.

Discussion Questions for Planning Teams

1. How would you say that climate in the church has changed over the last three to five years?
2. As you look to the future, where would you like the church to be on the climate MAPS discussed in previous chapters?
3. What are your hunches about the critical success factors for improving the climate in your congregation?
4. How will you go about confirming your hunches?
5. What might be the "least energy solution" traps you need to avoid?
6. How convinced are you that improving the climate in your congregation is a first step toward growing the church?

Discussion Questions for Middle Judicatory Leaders

1. How convinced are you that improving the climate in your congregations is a first step toward growing those churches?
2. How do you help congregations identify their organizational climate?
3. How would you help congregations identify the critical success factors for improving their climate?
4. What might be the "least energy solution" traps you need to help leaders avoid?

5. What are your hunches about the critical success factors for improving the climate in your middle judicatory?

Reflection for Consultants

1. How convinced are you that improving the climate in the congregations you serve is a first step toward growing those churches?
2. How do you help congregations identify their organizational climate?
3. How would you help congregations identify the critical success factors for improving their climate?
4. What might be the "least energy solution" traps you need to help leaders avoid?

Chapter 4

Culture and Growth

There are three indisputable facts related to the climate.

1. The CO^2 levels in the atmosphere are higher than they have been at any time in the last 400,000 years.
2. Ninety-seven percent of scientists believe that the global temperature has increased in the last 100 years.
3. Half of emperor penguins have disappeared in the last 50 years.

How human beings respond to these facts about the climate is a matter of human culture, and culture varies from one part of the world to another. While 77 percent of persons in Latin America and 60 percent of persons in Europe believe that climate change is harming people now, only 41 percent of people in the United States would agree. The culture in the United States makes it much less likely that the general population will make changes in response to the facts of climate change.

Church culture has a similar impact upon congregations and their growth or decline.

To illustrate this point, here is the story of two additional churches, Precipice Presbyterian and Heart Strong Methodist. Both have similar facilities, both are in the same community, and both have made reaching new people a priority. Both have good, but typical pastors, Mary and Marty.

Mary and Marty are good friends. One morning over coffee, they come up with the idea of holding a joint Easter service in the local high school auditorium. However, when Mary takes the idea to the session of Precipice Presbyterian it does not go well. The idea is tabled for a month. In that period of time, a few session members lobby with others in the congregation to get up a petition opposing the idea. By the time the next session meeting rolls around, it has become clear to Mary that the idea will create such a division within her church that she has to call Marty and back out of their plans. She has had a similar response to other proposed changes at the church such as a change in service times, rearranging the worship space, and adding a ramp at the entrance.

Over at Heart Strong Methodist, Marty's board has responded entirely differently. They are enthusiastic about the possibility of reaching people in the community. They proceed even though Precipice Presbyterian won't be joining them. Sure enough, the Easter service at the high school is twice as large as it was the previous year when it was held in the sanctuary. About a hundred of those attending were new people who by their own admission would not have attended an Easter service in a church.

What is the difference between these two churches? Culture.

Precipice Presbyterian has a HEARTH AND HOME culture described earlier. That means it has low flexibility. Its strength is maintaining important traditions. Its shadow side is becoming so system bound that any change, even promising ones, generate conflict.

Heart Strong Methodist has a PERFORMANCE culture. It has a similar theological perspective as Precipice, but a much higher degree of flexibility. Members are not only able to roll with change, they actually expect change.

As a result, the worship attendance at Heart Strong Methodist is growing at the rate of about 2 percent a year, while at Precipice Presbyterian worship attendance is declining about 4 percent a year. At that rate, in about five years Precipice Presbyterian will join the ranks of hundreds of other mainline churches when it will no longer be able to afford a full-time pastor.

Earlier, four different church cultures were introduced. See how each of these cultures exhibits tendencies to grow or decline (figure 8).[11] Don't let the names on this chart throw you. Just remember that more adaptable churches like Heart Strong are near the top of this chart and less flexible ones like Precipice are near the bottom.

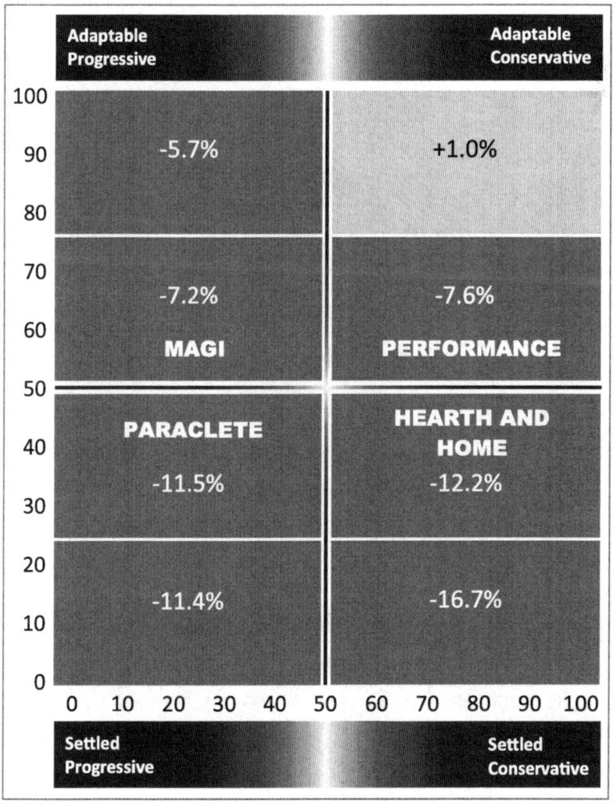

Figure 8 Growth and Decline for Different Cultures

What do we learn from this chart?

First, there is a clear relationship between church culture and changes in worship attendance. Specifically, there is significant downward pressure on worship attendance as the degree of flexibility decreases. The climate that is most hostile to church growth is HEARTH AND HOME.

Second, the most significant factor in a culture's impact on church growth is flexibility rather than theological perspective. As flexibility decreases, declines in worship attendance increase regardless of theological perspective. This means that simple theological prescriptions like "getting back to the Bible" or "becoming relevant" are not likely to impact church growth.

Third, only churches with cultures that are more conservative theologically *and* more flexible in their response to change are exhibiting growth as a group. The four-year rate of growth in worship attendance is small, but significant, about 1 percent per year. MAGI, PARACLETE, and HEARTH AND HOME quadrants all exhibit declines in worship attendance as a group.

Fourth, the positive impacts of flexibility do not really begin to kick in until it exceeds that of 75 percent of other churches. More theologically conservative churches with average flexibility are losing members at rates not that different from churches with low flexibility.

Finally, having a flexible culture does not guarantee that a church will grow, but having an inflexible climate almost guarantees that it won't. About half of the most adaptable focused churches are growing. Flexibility provides a foundation for growth strategies. It enables a church to make the changes necessary to realize its goals without generating a crippling amount of conflict. Of churches from HEARTH

AND HOME cultures, 87 percent are declining.

A little reflection at this point suggests why programs imported from other growing churches often don't work: They are not a good match for the culture. A program that works well in a PERFORMANCE culture will usually fail if applied in a PARACLETE culture . . . and vice versa.

More importantly, flexible cultures allow for experimentation, and the inevitable failure of some approaches, without penalizing their leaders. Experimentation allows churches to discover what will be effective in their particular community. This is especially important in a time when communities are extremely diverse and cookie cutter approaches usually do not work.

Circle back around to the opening example of Heart Strong Methodist. If their attempt to reach the community by moving the Easter service to the high school had resulted in mediocre attendance, a more adaptable culture would be willing to learn from the experience and move on. If the leaders were penalized for the attempt, a disincentive would be created for further experimentation. Future opportunities to discover what *is* effective are missed.

The chart makes it appear that more progressive churches cannot grow, even if they have high levels of flexibility. But the next chapter tells how both conservative and progressive churches can grow with attention to both shifting culture and managing the "shadow side."

Discussion Questions for Planning Teams

1. What surprises you in this chapter?
2. What would you estimate to be the theological perspective of your congregation compared to other congregations in your denomination? How diverse do you think the theological perspective is?
3. How flexible is your congregation compared to other congregations in your denomination?
4. How much freedom do leaders in your church have to try new approaches without being penalized?
5. From the information presented in this chapter, how likely is it that your church is going to be able to grow?
6. How important is it for members of your congregation to understand the culture of your church and how it might impede or support church growth?

Discussion Questions for Middle Judicatories

1. What surprises you in this chapter?
2. How many of the churches in your middle judicatory fall into each of the four quadrants described in this chapter?
3. Given this distribution, which churches are most likely to be growing?
4. Given this distribution, how long before the total worship attendance in your middle judicatory drops by half?

5. How self-aware are the members in your churches of their own culture and the positive/negative impacts of that culture on church growth?

Reflections for Consultants

1. What surprises you in this chapter?
2. How many of the churches you are now working with fall into each of the four quadrants described in this chapter?
3. How self-aware are the members in these churches of their own culture and the positive/negative impacts of that culture on church growth?
4. How important do you believe it is for the churches you are working with to be self-aware?

---

11 This chart seems to imply that more progressive churches can't grow. That is not the case. See chapter 5.

Chapter 5

Addressing Culture

My wife and I spent some time in Ireland several years ago, a country where cars drive on the left side of the road. We walked or took the bus nearly everywhere we went, so we didn't need a car. The adjustment for us was in simply crossing the street. When you cross a street in Ireland, your pattern of "looking" needs to change.

When you cross a street, the last direction you look is the direction traffic is coming from in the lane on your side of the street, because that's who would hit you as you step out. In the United States that means look left. As you walk across and before crossing the center line, you look right, because now those are the cars that would hit you. Look left; look right.

In Ireland you have to reverse that. Look right; look left. Sounds easy, right? Actually, it is not. Decades of habit have built an entire set of reflexes that need to be modified.

That is culture: a set of reflexes that cause you to react in certain ways without even thinking about it. Generally these reflexes speed decision-making in ways that protect or enhance life. The problem is that when the world changes, they are no longer helpful. They may even be harmful. What keeps you safe in the United States can get you run over in Ireland.

Aspects of church culture that once advanced the church's mission can now lead to the church's demise. What is required is one of the most difficult undertakings for a congregation: shifting its culture.

Culture Shifting

In chapter 3 the MAP for First Church (figure 7) indicates that members had successfully created a more positive climate resulting in numerical growth. In order to accomplish that growth, the members also had significantly shifted the culture in two ways (figure 9).

1. They moved theologically from moderately progressive to moderately conservative.
2. They moved from moderately adaptable to highly adaptable.

Overall, they moved from a region of the MAP where churches generally lose about 2 percent a year in worship attendance to a region where churches generally gain a small amount in worship attendance.

Entire books have been written on shifting organizational culture, and any reader would benefit from an online search for resources. In this chapter, I simply want to address the issue of missional flexibility—*the ability of a church to make the changes necessary to achieve its mission without having to invest a significant amount of energy in managing conflict.*

A lack of flexibility is often the underlying cause of many different problems that tend to occur over and over again.

- Problems with expectations regarding the pastor, especially when there is a pastoral change.
- Problems with decisions made by the governing board.
- Problems with changes in worship such as service times, music, or style.
- Problems with the education and formation ministries,

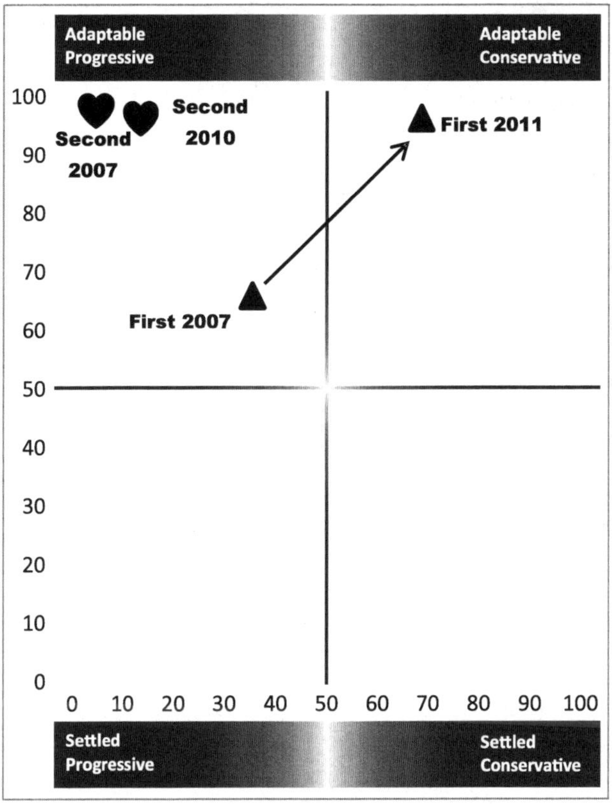

Figure 9 The Effect of Culture Change in Two Congregations

especially when there is a change in the curriculum or program.

- Problems with eliminating programs that are no longer effective.
- Problems with starting new programs to reach more people.
- Problems with decisions about the color, style, or placement of furnishings.
- Problems with changes in the use of building space.

- Problems with the allocation of financial resources or the approval of the budget.

Developing a flexible culture is critical to church health and growth. Three elements are key to making that shift.

First, there must be a distinction between mission and programs. Mission is primary. Programs are a means of accomplishing a mission, which makes them secondary. There are usually a hundred different ways of accomplishing a mission. Programs usually lock a congregation into one particular, often inflexible pathway.

As a pastor I was approached annually by the president of the women's association asking me to "fix" the declining membership in their organization by recruiting younger women into their ranks. I would regularly point out that the church had a robust ministry to younger women in the church through small groups of various kinds. The mission of the church relative to women was being accomplished but in a different way. I would then offer to help the association revamp their ministry to help it effectively reach younger women. The response was always the same: "Our program is set by the denomination. We can't change it."

Programs constrain. Mission liberates.

A congregation becomes more flexible when it can reflect in a non-anxious way on every aspect of its ministry and ask two questions.

1. What is our mission of this ministry?
2. What are alternative ways we could accomplish this mission?

Second, flexibility is learned by *doing* not by *thinking*. It is important to realize that there are things (like riding a bicycle, playing a piano, or dancing a waltz) you cannot learn from a discussion, debate, or reading a book. You have to try it. As someone said, you often can't think yourself into a new way of acting; you have to act into a new way of thinking.

Other aspects of "doing change" include.

- Adopt a "let's try it" attitude. Make change an experiment to see what works . . . and what doesn't. If you are not making some mistakes, generally you are not learning fast enough.

- Give change time. Many initial, apprehensive feelings tend to ease with time.

- Assume good motives on the part of leaders. You may or may not agree with some changes, but don't jump to the wrong conclusion without seeking to understand.

- In your life, do something different every day that makes you feel a "little" awkward.

- Seek resources that will help you understand why changes are needed in the church today and the kinds of changes that are likely to bear fruit.

- Be aware of your own change profile and how that tends to affect the way you deal with change.

- Read and meditate upon passages of Scripture dealing with change, such as the Israelites on the wilderness journey and Jesus in his transition from being a carpenter to becoming an itinerate preacher.

- Ask for help from others during change and offer positive encouragement to others who may be struggling.

Finally, developing flexibility, like any culture change, requires leadership with a particularly heavy dose of courage. Even the most well-managed change process will elicit a level of dissatisfaction. Some persons are likely to leave the fellowship. Making sure that clergy who are leading culture change have adequate support from fellow clergy, middle judicatories, and skilled consultants is essential to both wellness and effectiveness.

Keeping Your Culture . . . and Still Growing?

It is not impossible for less flexible cultures to grow. As mentioned earlier, only about 13 percent of churches in the less flexible regions of the MAP are reporting increases in worship attendance. HEARTH AND HOME or PARACLETE cultures can still grow, but it requires an intentional effort to manage their shadow sides.

A similar issue exists for churches with MAGI cultures.

On the whole, progressive churches with high flexibility are also losing members. An example is Second Church shown on the chart in chapter 3 (figure 7). Growth in worship attendance at Second Church dropped by two thirds over four years, while the climate deteriorated from TRANSFORMATIONAL to CHAOS.

On the culture MAP in this chapter (figure 9), there has been little shift in the flexibility of this church largely because its flexibility is higher than in nearly every other church in its community. Here the issue is likely not about shifting the culture, but managing the culture's shadow side.

Every church culture has a "shadow side" that (1) undermines the mission and (2) is largely unconscious to the members of the congregation. The reason the shadow side is unconscious to members is because it is generally the flip side of a set of strengths that has helped the church excel in one way or another.

One of the questions prompted by the research is this: Why is it that MAGI churches as a group have declining worship attendance (-5.7 percent) even at the highest levels of flexibility? I believe that part of the answer lies in their shadow side, so the next section focuses on the shadow side of the three cultures that, as a group, are not growing.

The Shadow Side of MAGI Cultures

Churches with a MAGI culture are more progressive with higher degrees of flexibility. This gives these churches a number of strengths that serve them well including:

- Curiosity
- Inclusiveness
- Advocacy
- Conceptualization

Conversely, MAGI cultures have a shadow side.[12] While they are inclusive, their more cerebral approach to faith can contribute to an emotionally arid atmosphere that can lead to lower scores on hospitality. In fact, those MAGI churches that have found a way to have higher levels of hospitality have positive four-year growth rates of about 3 percent.

Also, the intellectual curiosity of MAGI congregations can make it difficult for them to define exactly what they believe. This is in marked contrast to their cousins on the more conservative side of the chart who can state with some precision what they believe.

In addition, they can be so committed to being inclusive that it becomes challenging for them to develop clarity regarding their mission and vision. I have literally seen MAGI churches spend two years trying to discern their mission, only to give up in frustration because any degree of focus is going to exclude a particular population within the congregation.

Both of these strengths turned weaknesses can make it hard for a MAGI church to communicate who they are to their community in any way that makes them distinct from the faith communities around them. While they may not be dropping in worship attendance as fast as less flexible cultures, their four-year worship attendance numbers are negative for the group as a whole. Even though their number one priority is reaching new members, the shadow side of their culture is impeding their efforts.

For these churches, the challenge is not to shift culture, but to manage its shadow side. For a MAGI culture that can mean taking one or more of the following steps.

- Acknowledge the shadow side of the culture and seek to learn about it. At what point does inclusion become diffusion of mission? At what point does advocacy become a distraction from intrapersonal and interpersonal relationships? When does intellectual exploration become intellectualism, that is, a defense mechanism to avoid painful emotions?

- Enlist the aid of a trained facilitator who can skillfully guide the leadership in developing a vision, a mission statement, core values, and strategic values that (1) give expression to the central identity of the congregation and (2) distinguish the congregation from other congregations in the community.

- Articulate a clear path for spiritual development, how the Christian journey begins, what disciplines are important, and what mileposts of growth can be used to gauge progress.

- Develop the capacity of members to tell faith stories in ways that feel natural and invitational to others.

- Use sermons, liturgy, and education to develop the

capacity for members to be emotionally available to one another.

By taking a combination to steps that effectively address climate, culture shifts, and shadow sides, most MAGI churches can grow.

The Shadow Side of HEARTH AND HOME Cultures

Because HEARTH AND HOME cultures understand themselves as guardians of traditional understandings and practices, the positions they take may leave them open to the charge that they are simply resistant to change. The drive for spiritual and moral clarity on core issues may manifest itself in a lack of tolerance with one another, making them vulnerable to demoralizing conflicts. Their tendency to focus on the concrete side of matters may lead to inordinate attachments to facilities and furnishings. If they lose their missional focus, they may retreat into a fortress mentality and find themselves becoming a diminishing, aging congregation.[13]

For HEARTH AND HOME churches that do not want to shift culture, there are a number of steps that need to be taken to manage their shadow side.

Acknowledge the shadow side of the culture and seek to learn about it. At what point does a commitment to a particular tradition become a barrier to new people who cannot understand it? At what point does standing up for one's beliefs become divisive and disruptive? What is the church's history related to conflict?

Systematically train the congregation in skills that will help mitigate the debilitating effects of unmanaged conflict, including listening skills and conflict management skills.

Wherever possible, adopt a strategy of "bless and add," which means wherever possible, maintain existing ministries with little change while adding ministries that have more flexibility.

Where change is absolutely necessary, introduce it slowly and connect it to the historical DNA of the congregation.

The Shadow Side of PARACLETE Cultures

If PARACLETE cultures do not find a way to balance their openness with reasonable expectations of others, they may end up attracting more needs than the resources required to address those needs. Their admirable tendency to accept people where they are may not offer an adequate level of accountability that is also essential to wholeness. In addition, their traditions may become detached from everyday living and fail to achieve a practical, redemptive purpose.[14]

- Acknowledge the shadow side of the culture and seek to learn about it. At what point does a commitment to a particular tradition become a barrier to new people who cannot understand it? At what point does inclusion of ideas become diffusion of mission? When does unconditional acceptance sacrifice the accountability required for personal and organizational growth?

- Articulate a clear path for spiritual development, how the Christian journey begins, what disciplines are important, and what mileposts of growth can be used to gauge progress.

- Where change is absolutely necessary, introduce it slowly and connect it to the historical DNA of the congregation.

- Use sermons, liturgy, and education to help members understand how the church's traditions connect to everyday living and healing of the soul sick.

Putting It All Together

I became the pastor of a large church in the fall of 1984. The church had lost about 750 members over a fifteen-year period of time. One of my first meetings was with the evangelism committee. The governing board had assigned to the evangelism committee the task of recruiting fifty new members in the next year. This is the way that many churches view the work of evangelism: recruiting new members.

The research is clear. Church growth is first a matter of creating a certain kind of church, and only secondarily a matter of recruiting new members. As seen in the data, "typical" churches are not growing; in fact, they are losing members. The churches that tend to be growing are those where members are having extraordinary experiences, are highly satisfied and energized (transformational), demonstrate deep care for one another as well as concern for the needs of those yet to walk in the door, and are able to try new approaches to ministry without fear of penalty for failure.

This only makes sense. Churches that offer extraordinary experiences create "raving fan" members who naturally become evangelists in conversation with others. Developing the programs that will equip and deploy them, as well as the general marketing initiatives that expose the community to the church and its ministries is secondary.

What if a church doesn't want to take steps to either shift its culture or manage its shadow side? That is the question addressed in the final chapter.

Discussion Questions for Planning Teams

1. What surprises you in this chapter?
2. What would you identify as some of the "reflexes" of your congregation? How do those reflexes help or hinder your efforts to reach new members?

3. Review the list of problems caused by low flexibility in a congregation (page 54). Which of those is your congregation experiencing?
4. How would a greater willingness to experiment benefit your congregation's mission? How would a greater willingness to experiment potentially impede your congregation's mission?
5. How does the culture in your congregation need to change if you are to reach new members?

Discussion Questions for Middle Judicatories

1. What surprises you in this chapter?
2. Estimate the number of churches in your middle judicatory that have cultures that seriously sabotage their ability to reach new members. What are some common characteristics that these congregations share?
3. How are you currently helping congregations shift their cultures?
4. What role might middle judicatories play in helping congregations address culture issues?

Reflections for Consultants

1. What surprises you in this chapter?
2. How do you recognize when the culture of a congregation needs to change in order for them to reach new members?
3. How do you help churches shift their culture?
4. How do you help churches manage the shadow side of their cultures?

12 Crabtree, J. Russell, Owl Sight, Evidence-Based Discernment and the Promise of Organizational Intelligence for Ministry (Magi Press, 2012), 118.

13 Crabtree, J. Russell, Owl Sight, Evidence-Based Discernment and the Promise of Organizational Intelligence for Ministry (Magi Press, 2012), 115.

14 Crabtree, J. Russell, Owl Sight, Evidence-Based Discernment and the Promise of Organizational Intelligence for Ministry (Magi Press, 2012), 117.

Chapter 6

Getting Honest

Can we handle the truth? Here is the truth.

Truth #1 Emperor penguins and mainline Protestants are in serious decline. Penguin populations are projected to decline by another 50 percent by the year 2100. Two-thirds of mainline Protestant churches are experiencing long-term decreases in worship attendance. At this rate, they will decline another 80 percent by the year 2100.

Truth #2 The more a church declines, the more likely it is to decline further. Half of all churches with more than 1,000 persons in worship are growing. A third of churches with 500 persons in worship are growing. Only one in four churches with fewer than 100 persons in worship is growing. As a group, churches with fewer than 50 persons in worship are declining the fastest.

Truth #3 Distinctions between "quality" and "quantity" in churches are artificial. Churches where people are having positive experiences are much more likely to be growing. Churches where people are having more negative experiences are almost certain to be declining.

Truth #4 With the right changes in climate and culture, most churches can grow.

Truth #5 Absent concrete steps to manage climate and culture, no amount of planning, programs, money, or other resources will halt the decline in worship attendance.

Given these realities, an opportunity has opened up for local church leaders, middle judicatory leaders, and church consultants. Churches can become vital, growing, and effective in fulfilling the mission that God has given through Jesus Christ. But these leaders face significant choices.

Without major changes, most churches are going to continue to decline. Many churches are going to close.

However, change is difficult. When confronted with the choice between making these changes and closing in the near future, many members will respond by saying, "If we make all these changes, the church will no longer be recognizable to us. Either way we lose our church. We might as well have the church we love for as long as we can, and then leave something for the future of our community."

Strategically, this would be the *legacy* option. The legacy option is to not simply plan for closing, but to maximize the impact of the church in the years of ministry that remain and beyond. Legacy options include (a) making the building available to worthy causes, (b) selling the building and offering the proceeds to support other ministries, or (c) injecting the resources of the church into another community ministry through a merger.

A legacy strategy stands in direct opposition to a *survival* strategy. A survival strategy seeks resources simply to prolong a church's life. While a legacy strategy offers resources to the larger community, a survival strategy absorbs resources, often from the middle judicatory. As a matter of stewardship, churches are called to intentionally decide between the climate and cultural changes required for growth or to develop a legacy strategy. A survival strategy that eschews change while absorbing resources is a failure of discipleship.

The larger the church, the more promising is the adoption of a growth strategy. Churches must not wait until they are wrestling with downsizing thresholds like elimination of staff, invasion of rainy day funds, deferred maintenance, or leasing out building space before they take action.

This is especially important for middle judicatory strategy. Many middle judicatories today can reasonably predict that 10–20 percent of their churches will face closure in the next twenty years. A legacy strategy should be cultivated among those churches.

However, simply mitigating loss is not enough. Now is the time for middle judicatories to work strategically with their larger churches to cultivate strategies that will help them make the climate and cultural changes necessary for vitality and growth.

Jesus said, "You will know the truth, and the truth will make you free."[15]

I saw a poster once that had a rag doll going through a wringer. At the top it said, "The truth will set you free . . . "

At the bottom it said, ". . . but first it will make you miserable."

There is a freedom in knowing that we are not simply the victims of some mysterious downward force that is bleeding out the energy and zest of our faith communities. We have choices, and therein lies the suffering. Singing the new song of Psalm 96 falls easily from our lips as a concept, but new songs require creativity mixed with a tolerance for awkwardness and a thirst for adventure.

The question "How do we reach new members?" is not a bad question, but it is the second question. The first question is "How do we create a better church?" Specifically, how do we create a church . . .

- Where the soul sick find healing rather than silence or denial.
- Where spiritual practices become resources to address the real issues that people face in their lives.
- Where people find their best selves tapped in ways that empower them to make a meaningful contribution to the world.
- Where conflict becomes a means toward better solutions rather than further wounding.
- Where intellectual explorers are equipped with a faith that has plausibility in the contexts where they live and work.

The decline in mainline churches and the resultant quest for reaching new members may be a great gift to the church—provided it is understood as an opportunity to rethink how we do church and not simply as an enlistment campaign that allows churches to remain mired in an uncreative status quo.

Author Tyler Cowen argues that people have grown more risk averse and are reluctant to switch jobs or move to another state, and the desire to innovate—to grow and change—has gone away. In his book *The Complacent Class: The Self-Defeating Quest for the American Dream* he writes:

> Americans are in fact working much harder than before to postpone change, or to avoid it altogether, and that is true whether we're talking about corporate competition, changing residences or jobs, or building things. In an age when it is easier than ever before to dig in, the psychological resistance to

change has become progressively stronger.[16]

If the desire to grow and change has gone or is going away, the church of Jesus Christ should be the last to let it go, not the first. Penguins, Protestants, and many more of God's creatures now hang in the balance.

Discussion Questions for Planning Teams

1. How hard was it for you to read this chapter?
2. Discuss these three strategic options for your church.
    a. A growth strategy—making changes in climate and culture.
    b. A legacy strategy—planning for the ministry of the church to transition into other forms.
    c. A survival strategy—seeking resources to extend the life of the church as long as possible.

Discussion Questions for Middle Judicatories

1. How would you describe your middle judicatory strategy for its congregations in terms of growth, legacy, and survival?
2. Into which strategies are you investing most of your time and energy? How would you like to see that change?
3. Do you feel you are being honest with your congregations? Do you feel they are being honest with themselves?
4. If there are not changes, where is your middle judicatory headed?

Reflections for Consultants

1. How honest do you feel you are being with the congregations you are working with? How honest are they being with themselves?
2. What are the strategies being adopted by the churches you are working with? Growth (with change)? Legacy? Survival?
3. How might this chapter change the way you work with a church of 1,000 members? A church of 500 members? A church of 100 members? A church of 50 members?

---

15 John 8:32

16 Cowen, Tyler, The Complacent Class: The Self-Defeating Question for the American Dream (New York: St. Martin's Press, 2017),

About the Author

J. Russell Crabtree is an Ohio native and graduate of the Ohio State University with a degree in engineering physics. He worked in research at the Eastman Kodak Company for three years in the area of optics and electrostatic control systems. He left industry to attend seminary and served as a pastor for twenty years. He has worked in the field of organizational intelligence for thirty years, and served as a consultant for nearly twenty years.

Russ has authored numerous books. He lives with his wife, Shawn, in Hendersonville, North Carolina. Together, they have six children and twelve grandchildren.

For further information contact:

J. Russell Crabtree
Crows Feet Consulting
614-208-4090
russ@crowsfeetconsulting.com